A is for Airplane

An Aviation Alphabet

Written by Mary Ann McCabe Riehle and Illustrated by David Craig

Sleeping Bear Press™
310 North Main Street, Suite 300
Chelsea, MI 48118
www.sleepingbearpress.com

© 2009 Sleeping Bear Press is an imprint of Gale, a part of Cengage Learning.

Printed and bound in China.

First Edition

10 9 8 7 6 5 4 3 2 1

Library of Congress Cataloging-in-Publication Data

Riehle, Mary Ann McCabe, 1959-
A is for airplane : an aviation alphabet / written by Mary Ann McCabe
Riehle ; illustrated by David Craig.
p. cm.
Summary: "History, famous people, and types of aircraft are introduced
in this alphabet book. Topics include crew, dirigible, Amelia Earhart,
F-16s, helicopters, and John F. Kennedy"—Provided by publisher.
ISBN 978-1-58536-358-2
1. Aeronautics—Juvenile literature. I. Craig, David. II. Title.
TL547.R49 2009
 629.1—dc22   2008037623

To Bridget, Ellen, and Paul,
the wind beneath my wings.

MARY ANN

To the memory of my mum, Doreen Craig,
who passed away while I was painting this book.

DAVID

A a

Airplanes have made it possible for us to travel faster than with many other types of transportation. Airplanes are not only fast but are considered to be one of the safest ways to travel. Millions of flights a year carry billions of passengers from place to place. A trip from New York to Los Angeles would take over forty hours by car. Depending on the winds, the nearly 2,800 miles can be covered in about five hours by airplane.

Passenger travel in airplanes had its beginnings in Florida in 1914. For five dollars, a person could take the twenty-three minute flight from St. Petersburg to Tampa. The same trip by boat would take two hours. Unfortunately, the pilot could take only one passenger at a time. Today some airplanes carry more than five hundred passengers and can travel at speeds over five hundred miles per hour.

Want to travel in an amazing way?
Get on board with letter A.
An Airplane, of course, can get you there,
flying quickly through the air.

B is for Birds and their inspiration
for all things related to aviation.
It began when people watched birds fly
and then decided to give it a try.

It seems as if people have admired and tried to imitate the flight of birds throughout history. An attempt to fly like a bird is even part of Greek mythology. The story of Icarus who wore wax wings covered in feathers in order to fly away from the king ends tragically. The myth explains that because Icarus flew too high and got too close to the sun his wings melted and he fell to the sea.

During the eleventh century an English monk put wings on his arms and on his feet and tried to fly from the tower of his monastery. Not surprisingly, he broke both of his legs. Flight requires much more than flapping your wings.

It wasn't until the late 1400s that an artist, Leonardo da Vinci, seemed to understand people could not fly on their own but would need some type of machine to help them stay in the air. He designed and drew flying machines that would eventually become the basis for some of the earliest helicopters and airplanes.

Bb

Congratulations to letter **C** and the Crew
on the work and special tasks that they do.
Both on the ground and in the air
they do their jobs and show they care.

C c

The crew of a flight consists of more than just those who fly the airplane. From the baggage handlers that meet you at the curb to the flight attendants that greet you on board, and all those airport workers in between, it's easy to see that it takes many people working together for a successful flight. Once aboard the plane the flight attendants not only strive to make the passengers comfortable but are also an important part of the safety procedures on board. Members of the ground crew refuel and load the plane and mechanics take care of any maintenance that is required. Cleaning crews make sure the airplane is tidy and ready for the next group of passengers. Another important group of people work from the control tower at the airport making sure that all of the planes take off and arrive safely. It takes many people to get a plane ready for takeoff and to take care of it after it lands.

Dirigibles were built in Germany and flown by Count Ferdinand von Zeppelin in the early 1900s. His first flight included five passengers and lasted approximately twenty minutes. These airships were able to be controlled and directed but were filled with extremely flammable gases such as hydrogen. One of aviation's most devastating disasters involving a dirigible was the explosion of the *Hindenburg*. On May 6, 1937 after a transatlantic journey the *Hindenburg* caught fire as it approached its destination in Lakehurst, New Jersey.

Though passenger travel on dirigibles, also known as zeppelins, essentially ended in the late 1930s, uses for these unique flying machines continued to evolve. Today's blimps are not as rigid and the gases used are much safer than the earlier dirigible type airships. Blimps can often be seen flying over large sporting events, providing film coverage from high above the game, race, or match. Advertisers often use the blimps to promote their companies since they travel slowly and attract the attention of large groups of spectators.

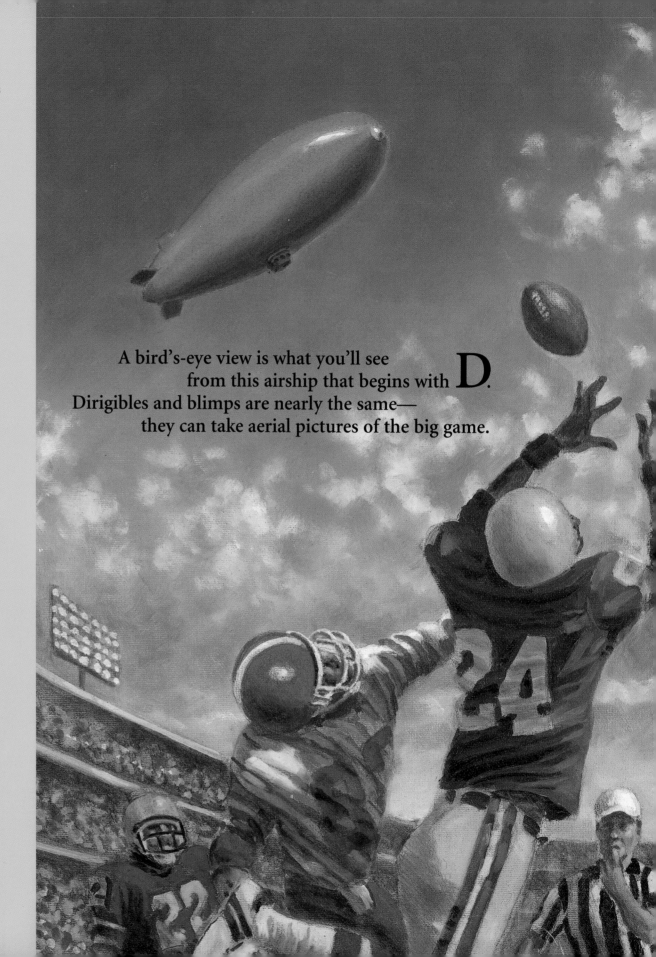

A bird's-eye view is what you'll see
from this airship that begins with D.
Dirigibles and blimps are nearly the same—
they can take aerial pictures of the big game.

Dd

E e

We dedicate the letter E
to a woman who went down in history.
Amelia Earhart was her name;
this flying female earned her fame.

In May of 1932 Amelia Earhart made history when she became the first woman to fly solo across the Atlantic Ocean. The Kansas-born Earhart flew from Newfoundland to Northern Ireland.

The following year Earhart was a guest at a White House dinner. That evening the First Lady of the United States, Eleanor Roosevelt, was treated to a flight over the nation's capital with America's "first lady of aviation," Amelia Earhart.

The U.S. Congress awarded Earhart the Distinguished Flying Cross. She was the first woman to receive this honor. Amelia Earhart served as the first president of an international organization of women pilots known as the "Ninety-Nines," named for its ninety-nine original members.

In an attempt to fly around the world in 1937, Earhart and her navigator, Fred Noonan, left New Guinea on July 2. While crossing the Pacific Ocean they lost radio contact. Though many people searched, the plane and its occupants were never found. Exactly what happened to Amelia Earhart still remains a mystery.

Letter F for this flying feat—
if you've ever seen one, it's pretty neat!
F-16s flying over in formation
can create quite a sensation.

F f

Flying airplanes in formation is a specialty that requires precision and tremendous skill. While at times it is important for military pilots to fly in tight formation for security and protection it is better known to the general public as a type of aerial entertainment.

Pilots in planes as close as three feet apart perform daring loops, rolls, acrobatic maneuvers, and various formations. The exciting display in the air is sometimes accented by colorful exhaust trails that are tinted to show up better in the sky.

The United States Air Force Thunderbirds flying the F-16 Fighting Falcon, the United States Navy pilots known as the Blue Angels, and England's Royal Air Force Red Arrows are some of the most renowned demonstration squadrons for this type of flying.

Before airplanes were powered by engines, aviation pioneers experimented with gliders. A glider is an unpowered plane that uses the wind and air currents to fly. The early gliders of Englishman Sir George Cayley resembled the shape of modern day aircraft. Otto Lilienthal, an engineer in Germany, was considered an expert with gliders. In 1891 Lilienthal began flying gliders and eventually was able to reach distances over nine hundred feet or further than three football fields. He piloted the gliders by hanging down from a harness and twisting his body, kicking his legs, and shifting his weight to guide them. Another pioneer, Octave Chanute depended on the steady winds that were often found over the sand dunes of Lake Michigan to complete many successful glider flights.

Gliding didn't end with powered flight. Gliders are still used for recreation, competition, and sport. Some gliders are towed into the air by powered airplanes and then released when the desired altitude and wind conditions are met. Hang gliding is enjoyed by enthusiasts and is very similar to Lilienthal's method involving the pilot in a harness beneath a fabric sail. Some pilots launch themselves by simply running down a steep hill and catching the wind at just the right moment.

Gg

A graceful Glider, that's two letter Gs
for an aircraft that floats with the breeze.
How high and far this type of plane goes
depends a lot on how the wind blows

H h

Helicopters can hover in one spot and can take off and land vertically. They don't need a runway. This makes the helicopter a very versatile aircraft. Helicopters are used in rescue missions and medical emergencies. Helicopters can deliver food, supplies, and people to remote places like oil rigs or to other locations with limited access. Helicopters can also be used by television and radio stations to report traffic conditions or to cover other news events from above the scene. Tourists can enjoy a helicopter ride and get a spectacular view of the city or area that they are visiting.

Helicopters come in various sizes from those intended to carry just a few passengers to ones large enough to carry troops and vehicles. Helicopters are able to fly forward, backward, and side to side. The wings of a helicopter are called rotors. The rotors look similar to the paddles on a ceiling fan. The main rotor blades spin very quickly and lift the helicopter off the ground. A smaller set of rotors on the tail keep the helicopter from spinning out of control. Igor Sikorsky built the first helicopter with a tail rotor in the 1930s.

H is here to save the day,
    helping those who are in harm's way.
Helicopters can hover and fly
    where a plane could not dare to try.

There is no limit, not even the sky
     with Imagination and the letter I.
Can you imagine some day taking a vacation
     to visit the International Space Station?

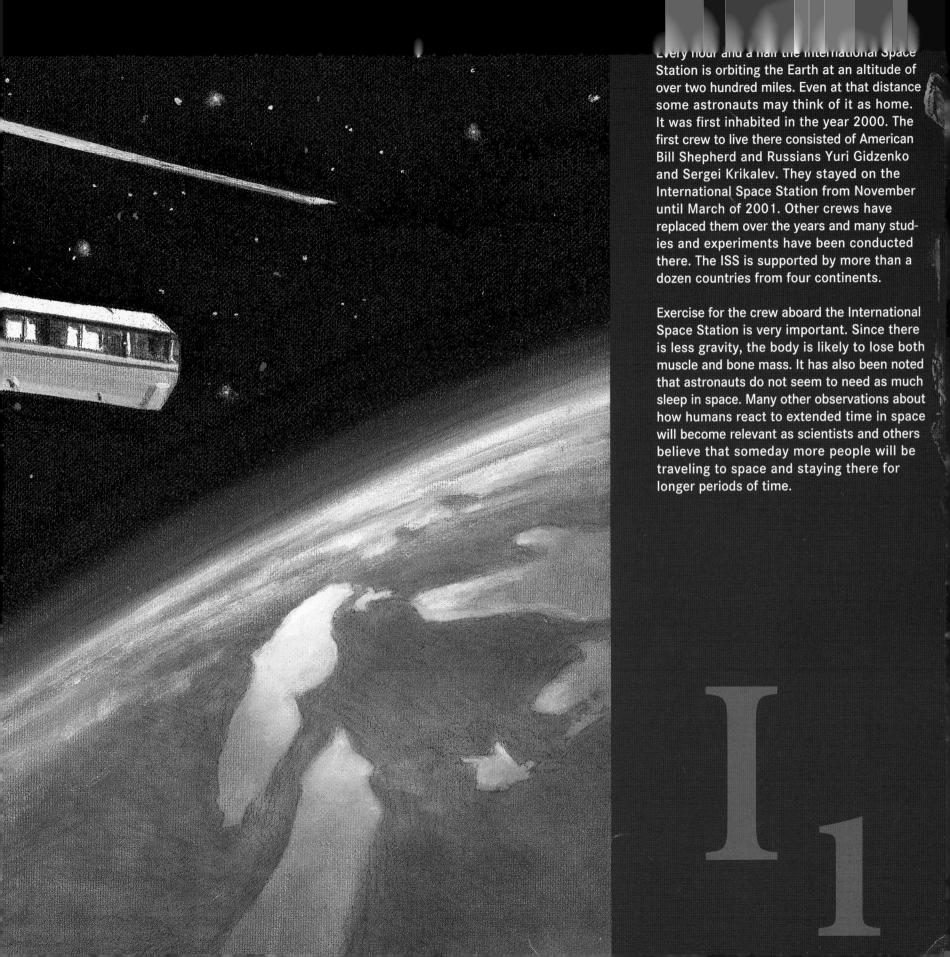

Every hour and a half the International Space Station is orbiting the Earth at an altitude of over two hundred miles. Even at that distance some astronauts may think of it as home. It was first inhabited in the year 2000. The first crew to live there consisted of American Bill Shepherd and Russians Yuri Gidzenko and Sergei Krikalev. They stayed on the International Space Station from November until March of 2001. Other crews have replaced them over the years and many studies and experiments have been conducted there. The ISS is supported by more than a dozen countries from four continents.

Exercise for the crew aboard the International Space Station is very important. Since there is less gravity, the body is likely to lose both muscle and bone mass. It has also been noted that astronauts do not seem to need as much sleep in space. Many other observations about how humans react to extended time in space will become relevant as scientists and others believe that someday more people will be traveling to space and staying there for longer periods of time.

In 1969 the Boeing 747 was the first airliner to be considered a "jumbo jet." The wingspan of a jumbo jet is nearly twice as long as the distance covered by the Wright brothers' first flight.

A jumbo jet can carry more than five hundred passengers but if a jumbo jet is flying longer distances it carries fewer passengers and more fuel. If it is traveling shorter distances it can carry less fuel and more people. The jumbo jet is wide enough to have ten passengers per row and two aisles. Boeing 747s have a partial upper deck that gives the central structure known as the fuselage a hump. This unique shape explains its nickname, "the whale."

Not only can a jumbo jet carry large amounts of people and cargo, a 747 is big enough to carry the space shuttle on its back and return it from California to its launch site in Florida.

Jumbo jets continue to get even larger. The Airbus A380 could even be considered a "superjumbo jet." Depending on the arrangement of the double-deck interior compartments, it can transport between 500 and 800 passengers and still have a third deck below for cargo. The jet is so large that only certain airports throughout the world are able to have the A380 take off and land in their airfields.

Up, up, and away
on a Jumbo Jet for letter J
With powerful engines there are many things jets do.
Jets can carry passengers and deliver cargo too.

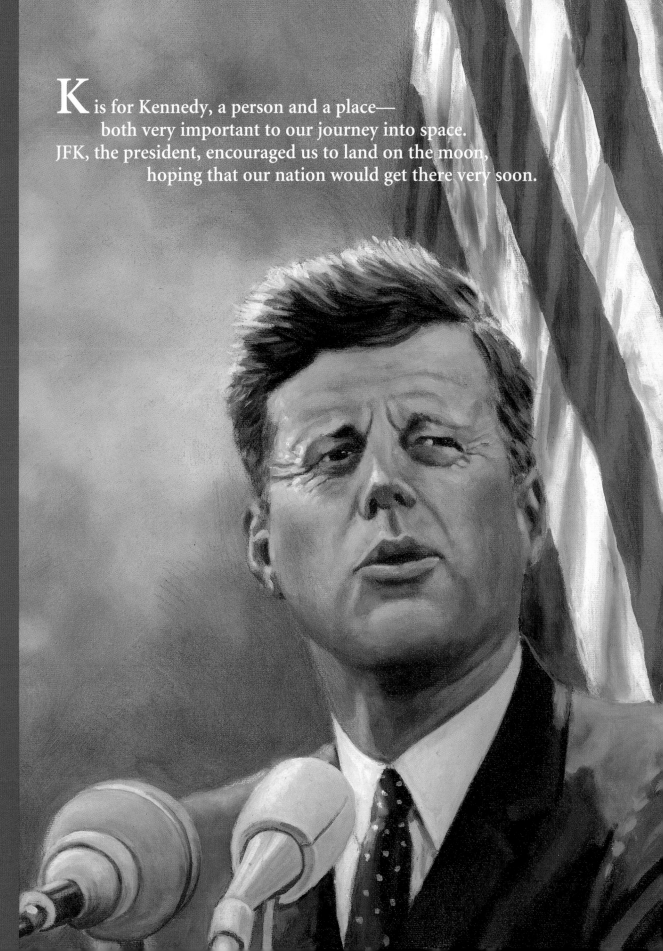

K is for Kennedy, a person and a place—
both very important to our journey into space.
JFK, the president, encouraged us to land on the moon,
hoping that our nation would get there very soon.

President John F. Kennedy spoke the following words to the United States Congress on May 25, 1961:

"I believe that this nation should commit itself to achieving the goal, before this decade is out, of landing a man on the moon and returning him safely to Earth."

America met the challenge. On July 20, 1969 Apollo 11's lunar module landed on the moon and Neil Armstrong and Buzz Aldrin walked on its surface. Since their safe return others have done the same, and space exploration continues as people discover new frontiers beyond the Earth's limits.

President Kennedy did not live long enough to see man walk on the moon but his commitment to space exploration is remembered each time a launch takes place at the John F. Kennedy Space Center named in his honor. The center near Cape Canaveral, Florida, formerly referred to as NASA's Launch Operations Center, was renamed for President Kennedy in November of 1963.

Charles Lindbergh was the first person to fly solo nonstop across the Atlantic Ocean. On May 20, 1927 Lindbergh took off from Roosevelt Field in New York. The plane carried over four hundred gallons of fuel. Lindbergh only brought along a quart of water and five sandwiches. After struggling to stay awake and dealing with bad weather conditions he landed in Paris, France. The flight took thirty-three hours and twenty-nine minutes. He had flown over 3,600 miles on that trip in the plane he named *Spirit of St. Louis* in thanks to the businessmen of that city who had supported him.

Charles had been interested in airplanes ever since he was a young boy growing up in Minnesota. His mother was a teacher and his father served as a U.S. Congressman from Minnesota.

Charles Lindbergh grew up to become an aviator and an author. Lindbergh told the story of his historic flight in a book entitled *The Spirit of St. Louis*. The book won the Pulitzer Prize in 1954.

"Lucky Lindy," that's letter L times two
for Charles Lindbergh who over the ocean flew.
Without stopping he took a chance
he could make it alone from New York to France.

Military Monument for the letter M–
a lasting tribute to honor all of them.
Men and women who serve from above
flying to protect the country they love.

The United States Air Force Memorial is
located on a hilltop in Arlington, Virginia. I
was dedicated in October of 2006 to hono
the men and women of the United States A
Force and members of the military organi
tions that came before it. The military did n
have any airplanes until purchasing one fro
the Wright brothers in 1909. The monumen
stands near the site where Orville Wright fle
that first plane sold to the U.S. military.

The monument took fifteen years to comple
but was ready in time for the 60th annive
sary of the United States Air Force officia
becoming a separate branch of the militar
It was designed by James Ingo Freed. The
architect was inspired by watching the Ai
Force's Thunderbirds precision team perfor
The monument features three metal spire
reaching to the sky and bending away as if
replicate one of the squadron's maneuve
The spires reach up to 270 feet in the air. Th
three spires symbolize the core values of th
Air Force: integrity, service, and excellence.

M
m

The National Air and Space Museum in Washington, D.C. houses the world's largest collection of historic airplanes and space-craft. It is part of the Smithsonian Institution. The National Air and Space Museum is visited by an average of nine million people a year.

The 1903 Wright brothers' *Flyer* and the U.S. Armed Forces first military plane the Wright *Military Flyer* are both on display at the museum.

Charles Lindbergh's *Spirit of St. Louis* is also on display. The Lockheed Vega flown by Amelia Earhart on her solo flight over the Atlantic Ocean is at the museum as well. These two historic flights took place exactly five years apart. Lindbergh flew May 20-21, 1927 and Amelia Earhart's solo flight took place May 20-21, 1932.

In 1986 Jeana Yeager and Dick Rutan flew around the world nonstop completing the flight in nine days. Their *Voyager* can also be seen at the National Air and Space Museum.

Artifacts from space flight such as the *Apollo 11* command module are also part of the impressive museum collection.

So much history in one place,
planes and rocket ships from outer space.
Now for the location, you'll be sure to see them:
N is for the National Air and Space Museum.

Oshkosh, Wisconsin draws aviation enthusiasts from all over the world as the host city of EAA AirVenture Oshkosh. Once known as the Experimental Aircraft Association's Fly-In Convention and still referred to as "The World's Greatest Aviation Celebration" the gathering began in 1953. It was first held in Milwaukee and later moved to Rockford, Illinois. As the event grew in popularity a larger location was needed and the city of Oshkosh was selected. The EAA agreed to move the event to Oshkosh in 1969.

Spectacular aerial demonstrations, historical and innovative aircraft displays, and the opportunity to attend workshops and learn more about aviation are some of the reasons more than 750,000 travel to Oshkosh each year.

Oshkosh is a city that begins with O;
   it's known to host an outstanding air show.
You can fly in or arrive by car
   joining the crowds from near and far.

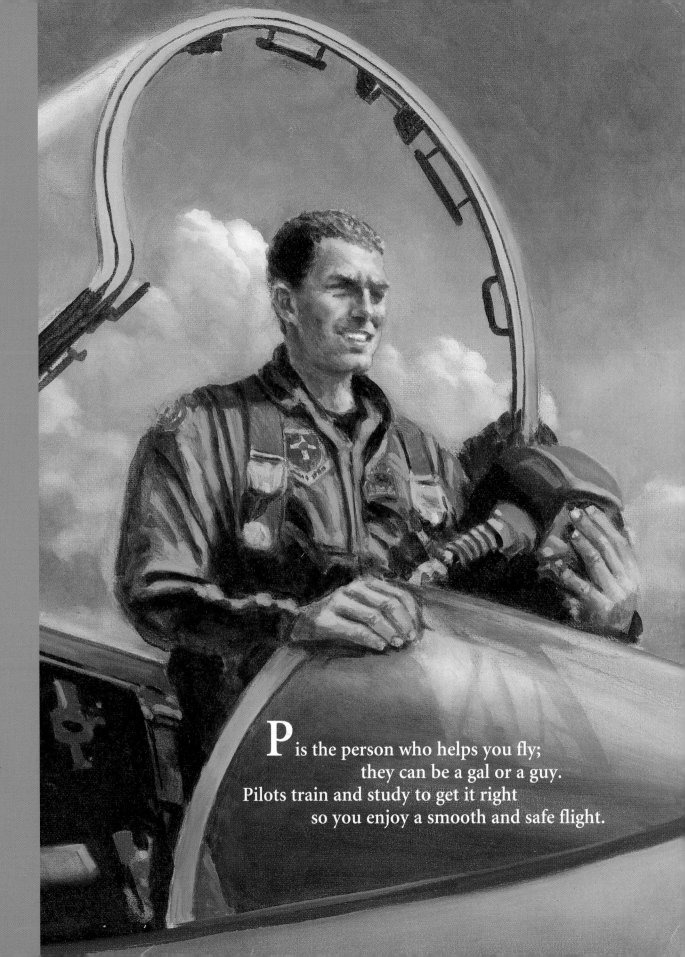

P p

Preparing to become a pilot takes a great deal of training and dedication. Some pilots are trained while serving in the military, others choose to train as civilians. Some colleges offer aviation related classes and majors. Technical schools and flight schools can also provide the initial training required.

Flying lessons can be expensive and many hours are required. Rental of an aircraft is also needed for instruction. Simulators are used to train future pilots how to handle various emergencies and flight situations. Two hundred and fifty hours of actual flight time are needed to obtain a commercial pilot certificate. Many tests are required even after that is earned. Pilots must know the English language since it is the official language of aviation and important for safety and communication with air traffic controllers. A language misunderstanding could result in a major mishap.

Extensive training continues even after a pilot is hired. Because a pilot has so much responsibility, the requirements are tough but the career can be very rewarding.

P is the person who helps you fly;
they can be a gal or a guy.
Pilots train and study to get it right
so you enjoy a smooth and safe flight.

Engineers have made significant advances i[n]
making airplanes quieter, both inside and
out. As with all aviation challenges, engineers continue to try to solve problems an[d]
improve on past solutions. New technolog[y],
materials, and engine design innovations
have made airplanes quieter.

A less technical way to reduce airplane nois[e]
that may be disturbing those on the groun[d]
is to put a curfew on flights. Many airports
do not allow planes to take off or land durin[g]
the late night or very early morning hours[.]
Some countries ban planes from taking off
and landing if they do not meet noise
standards.

As communities develop, airports are no
longer "out in the middle of nowhere."
Sensitivity to the noise levels generated by
air traffic has prompted the airline industr[y]
and government on the local and nationa[l]
levels to deal with the issue of noise pollutio[n].
Community organizations are also involve[d]
monitoring their airports and advocating fo[r]
peace and quiet.

Quiet please for the letter Q
and the airplanes flying over you.
Engineers can be quite proud
they've designed engines that aren't so loud.

Does an airplane ever seem like a car?
Perhaps when it's traveling on our word for **R**.
Runways are roads where aircraft drive
when they take off and when they arrive.

R r

Runways are the pathways that airplanes use to take off from and land on at an airport. Runways can be various lengths depending on the needs of and types of aircraft using them. The Federal Aviation Administration or FAA determines the minimum length for runways depending on the size of the airplanes. Runways need to be as level as possible and well maintained.

Planes take their turns waiting on the runways until one is clear to take off. Air traffic controllers in the tall tower at an airport are in contact with the pilot and give permission for that flight to take off or land on a specific runway. The runways are marked with numbers and are lit at night or when weather conditions make it difficult to see.

The space shuttle is intended to launch into space, repair or deliver satellites, perform various tasks, and return to Earth, landing on a runway like an airplane. After all of that is accomplished, the space shuttle is able to be reused for another mission.

The space shuttle program began on April 12, 1981 with the launch of *Columbia STS-1*. The first shuttle was launched in Florida and landed at Edwards Air Force Base in California. Astronauts Robert Crippen and John Young manned the flight. Within a year that space shuttle was back in space on another mission.

Crews on the earliest shuttles were limited to two astronauts. Later missions increased the size of the crew by adding mission specialists to take care of the space shuttle and payload specialists to take care of the experiments on board. A member of the *STS-7* space shuttle crew in 1983, Sally Ride, became the first American woman in space.

S s

What takes off like a rocket and lands like a plane
and then gets ready to do it all over again?
The Space Shuttle is that special spacecraft, and yes
it is the selection for letter S.

The Tuskegee Airmen were America's first black military airmen. Trained in Tuskegee, Alabama, nine hundred and ninety-four pilots graduated at the Tuskegee Army Air Field between1942 and 1946. These pilots came from all across America and served their country during World War II.

Tuskegee Airmen flew thousands of missions overseas but had to face other types of battles in their homeland and abroad. Prejudice and racism made life difficult for the Tuskegee Airmen. They were military officers but they were not allowed into officers' clubs on military bases. They were not treated as equals in many other ways.

Even though the Tuskegee Airmen were very qualified and well trained, a segregation policy kept the black airmen from serving in other units. Eventually that policy was abolished. In 1948 President Truman gave orders that ended the segregation in the military.

Tt

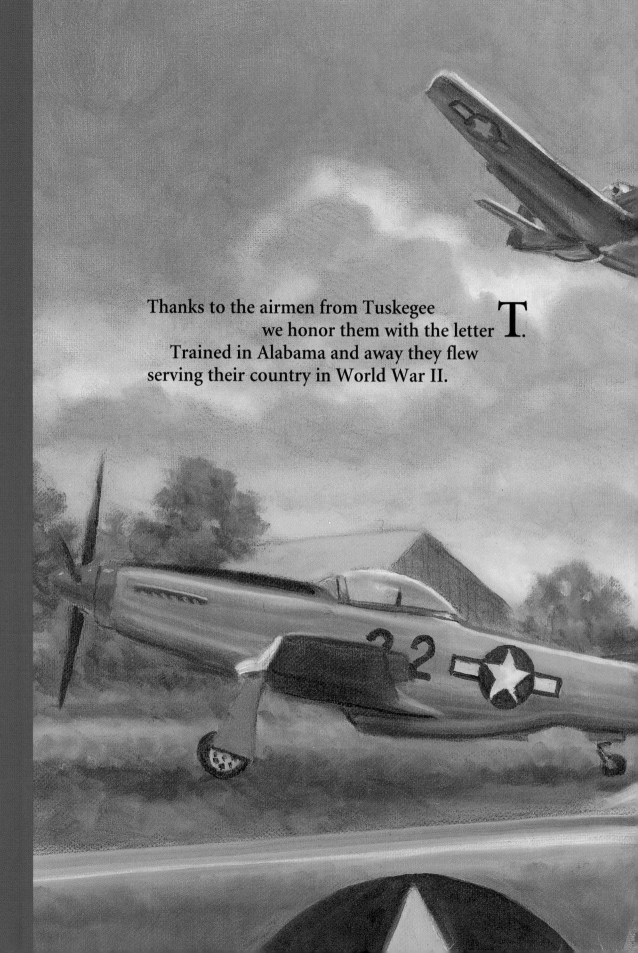

Thanks to the airmen from Tuskegee
we honor them with the letter T.
Trained in Alabama and away they flew
serving their country in World War II.

The undercarriage, or landing gear of an aircraft is determined by the type of landing surface. Airplanes that land on smooth runways have wheels underneath. The wheels can be folded up and stored in the body of the plane while flying and then let back down again and locked into place in time for landing. The ability to store the wheels while flying helps cut down on wind resistance. Planes that take off and land on water use floats instead of wheels. Helicopters may have skids that look like skis mounted on the bottom. This helps them land on surfaces that may be rocky or uneven. Some airplanes can actually have skis attached to their wheels to travel in places that are often snow covered.

U is for Undercarriage,
a term that's easy to understand
for the floats or wheels supporting a plane
when on water or on land.

U u

V v

V is a very special letter
for something that makes a plane fly better.
Vertical stabilizer is the important part
that helps it fly straight, right from the start.

The vertical stabilizer is located at the rear of the fuselage. The vertical stabilizer is a fixed part, meaning that it does not move. A rudder on the vertical stabilizer can move. Its purpose is to control the position of the nose of the airplane.

The vertical stabilizer is sometimes called a vertical fin or tail fin. It helps keep the plane steady. Sometimes wind gusts or other conditions can cause an airplane to sway. The vertical stabilizer has been compared to the tail feathers on an arrow. Without the tail feathers the arrow would be unstable and possibly veer off course. The vertical stabilizer serves the same purpose by keeping the airplane stable and on the right course.

Can you name the brothers who
built a plane that finally flew?
If your answer was Wright, then you knew
the word for letter W.

The Wright brothers, Wilbur and Orville, opened the Wright Cycle Company in Dayton, Ohio in 1892 but it was the work done in the back room of that shop that led them to their place in aviation history. While repairing and selling bicycles they were also working on their invention of what would become the world's first powered and controlled aircraft.

They had studied the work of aviation pioneers before them and Wilbur even wrote to the Smithsonian Institution and requested as much information as he could get about flight.

With all of the information, the mechanical skills and the desire to fly, the brothers began to build model planes. They started by testing gliders but those require windy conditions not regularly found in Dayton. Wilbur and Orville moved their project to Kitty Hawk, North Carolina. It was there on December 17, 1903 with Orville as the pilot, that the first powered, controlled, sustained, manned flight took place. The brothers named their airplane the *Flyer*. That day it flew 120 feet for twelve seconds. It could be considered the most important flight in the history of aviation.

W
W

On a clear day you can sometimes see cloud-like lines in the sky that are caused by airplane traffic. These vapor trails or condensation trails are made of water vapor. The water condenses around the exhaust from the plane and forms these cirrus type clouds.

Contrails, short for condensation trails, can tell a lot about the atmosphere. A clear sky without contrails or very short ones means the upper atmosphere is drier than on a day with longer lasting trails.

X can appear out of the blue
and show you where two airplanes flew.
As if it were written in the sky
to mark the spot the planes passed by.

Yy

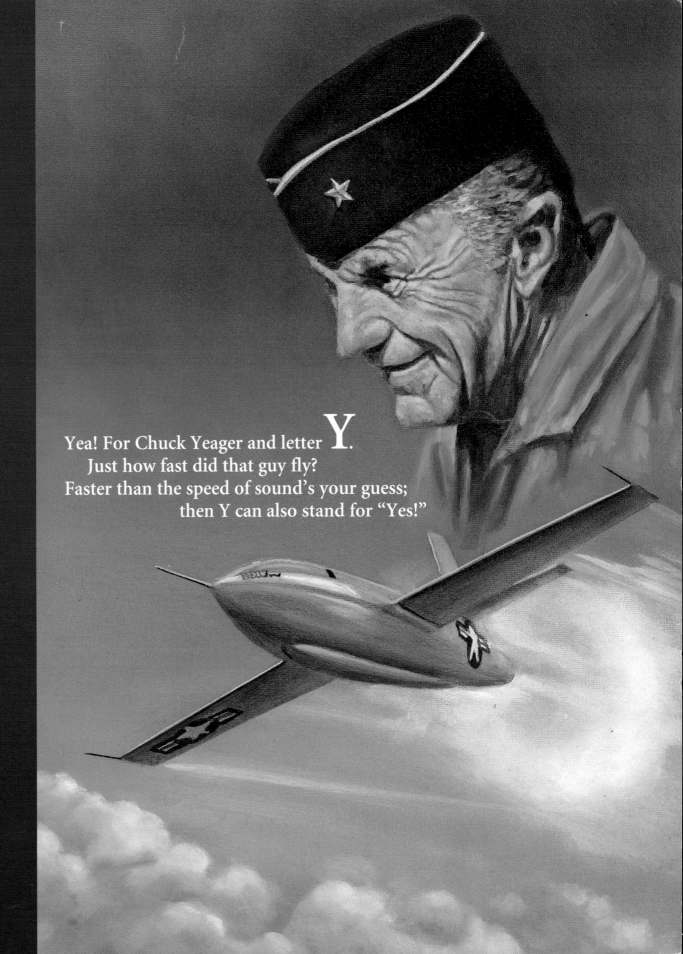

Yea! For Chuck Yeager and letter Y.
  Just how fast did that guy fly?
Faster than the speed of sound's your guess;
    then Y can also stand for "Yes!"

Flying a Bell X-1 on October 14, 1947, Chuck Yeager became the first pilot to fly faster than the speed of sound. A few years later in 1953, Yeager broke another record by flying two and a half times the speed of sound. Flights faster than the speed of sound are considered supersonic. Yeager has been referred to as "Mr. Supersonic."

The speed of sound, also called Mach 1, is approximately 760 miles per hour. It's an estimate because the measurement depends on the temperature and altitude.

Chuck Yeager, also known as Brigadier General Charles E. Yeager, was a fighter pilot in World War II. He retired from the military in 1975. Yeager Airport in his home state of West Virginia is named for him.

Zero gravity does not naturally occur on Earth, but scientists and others have found ways to create the experience of weightlessness.

Astronauts have trained for zero gravity conditions in simulators to prepare for space missions. Now businesses are beginning to offer people opportunities to take special flights aboard modified jets. These aircraft fly in a way that would make you feel like you're on a roller coaster, flying up and then diving down throughout the flight. The cabin is padded and passengers are able to float for a short time.

In April of 2007, astrophysicist Stephen Hawking, who has been confined to a wheelchair for almost forty years, was able to experience zero gravity, a concept he has studied most of his career. Aboard one of these special flights over the Atlantic Ocean just beyond the Kennedy Space Center, Hawking was able to leave his wheelchair. His nurses and physicians witnessed him doing a couple of flips and floating in the air. He was free to fly.

What would it feel like to float and be free?
Z You could find out with no gravity.
Z for Zero gravity and that uplifting feeling
when you rise up from the floor to the ceiling.

Z z

A Fuselage of Fun Facts

1. Which state first introduced passenger airplane travel?

2. Name the artist who sketched some of the earliest concepts of flying machines.

3. What are some of the duties of the ground crew?

4. What is a more common word for dirigible?

5. Name the first woman to fly solo across the Atlantic Ocean.

6. What is the name of the United States Navy formation flying demonstration squadron?

7. Name the German engineer considered a glider expert.

8. What are some differences between helicopters and airplanes?

9. In what year did astronauts begin living in the International Space Station?

10. Name the airliner first considered to be a jumbo jet.

11. When did *Apollo 11* land on the moon?

12. What did Charles Lindbergh name the plane that he flew solo nonstop across the Atlantic Ocean?

13. Where is the United States Air Force Memorial?

14. Name the museum that houses the largest collection of planes and spacecraft.

15. Which Wisconsin city hosts an annual air show known as "The World's Greatest Aviation Celebration"?

16. What is the official language of aviation?

17. Why do some airports ban airplanes from taking off and landing late at night or very early in the morning?

18. Who clears an airplane for takeoff?

19. Name the first American woman in space.

20. Where were the Tuskegee Airman trained?

21. Name more than one type of undercarriage for aircraft.

22. What is another term for an airplane's tail fin?

23. What year did the Wright brothers accomplish the first powered, controlled, manned flight?

24. What is another word for condensation trail?

25. Name the pilot who first flew faster than the speed of sound.

26. How do astronauts train for zero gravity conditions?

Answers

1. Florida
2. Leonardo da Vinci
3. Fuel the plane, load luggage
4. Blimp
5. Amelia Earhart
6. Blue Angels
7. Otto Lilienthal
8. Helicopters don't require runways. Helicopters can hover in one spot.
9. 2000
10. Boeing 747
11. July 20, 1969
12. *Spirit of St. Louis*
13. Arlington, Virginia
14. The National Air and Space Museum

15. Oshkosh
16. English
17. This helps decrease the noise and disturbance for people living near the airport.
18. Air traffic controller
19. Sally Ride
20. Tuskegee Army Air Field in Tuskegee, Alabama
21. Wheels, floats, skids, skis
22. Vertical stabilizer
23. 1903
24. Contrail or vapor trail
25. Chuck Yeager
26. They practice and get used to the feelings of weightlessness in a simulator.

Mary Ann McCabe Riehle

As a teacher, parent, and published author, Mary Ann McCabe Riehle has encouraged young students and adults to follow their dreams and tell their stories. She is a graduate of Xavier University with degrees in Communication Arts and Education. As a featured speaker at several reading and writing conferences, she emphasizes that "reading takes you places." She hopes that *A is for Aviation*, her third children's book, will encourage readers of all ages to reach new heights.

Mary Ann lives in Dexter, Michigan with her husband, Paul, and two daughters, Bridget and Ellen. While enjoying time in their yard with the family dog, Bisbee, they can see many of the aircraft featured in this book from small planes to jumbo jets.

David Craig

Illustrator David Craig has always loved creating pictures. As the son of a Canadian WWII pilot and a British Women's Auxiliary Air Force photographer, he grew up with aviation all around him. At home he was an avid history buff, and his drawings often depicted high-flying adventures featuring British World War II Spitfires. Today David still maintains those passions. "I love to tell a story with my pictures," David explains. "I like to create a mood. I want to put you there." He has illustrated several children's books including *First to Fly*, the story of the Wright brothers, which won the inaugural James Madison Book Award in 2003.

His remarkable skill at depicting historical events and people has led to projects as diverse as collectors' plates featuring images of World War II and a millennial champagne label illustrating moments from Canadian history. David lives in Mississauga, Ontario.